Strategic Habitat Conservation

A Report from the
National Ecological Assessment Team

~ June 29, 2006 ~

TABLE OF CONTENTS

PREFACE

Across the conservation community, species and habitat conservation increasingly rely on landscape approaches that integrate scientific information with management decisions. The tools and language of conservation are evolving, and using consistent and broadly understood methods will improve our ability to succeed.

Recognizing the changing field of conservation, both internal and external to the FWS, the Directorate chartered a cross programmatic effort in June, 2004 to: 1) characterize current and emerging scientific habitat conservation strategies and 2) recommend unifying approaches and capacity building measures (see Appendix A). The Team, featuring a mix of FWS and USGS technical and policy experts, focused on identifying how best to prioritize and make trust resource management decisions.

The National Ecological Assessment Team:	
Charles Baxter (R4), Rex Johnson (R9), and Clint Riley (R9)	Migratory Birds
Dirck Byler (R9), Rob Dietz (R2), John Esperance (R6), Mike Estey (R6), Steve Earsom (R4), Fred Paveglio (R1), and Jan Taylor (R5)	National Wildlife Refuge System
Deb Green (R9)	National GIS Coordinator
Wilson Laney (R4), Leopoldo Miranda-Castro (R9), and David Perkins (R5)	Fisheries and Habitat Conservation
Debby Crouse (R9)	Endangered Species
Craig Czarnecki (R3) and Stew Fefer (R5)	Ecological Services
Karene Motivans	NCTC
Anne Frondorf and Pat Heglund	USGS

We envision the FWS working collaboratively with partners to develop and implement a landscape approach to habitat conservation, leading to what we term *strategic habitat conservation*. Success will depend on how quickly and effectively our organizational approach evolves, including steps to better communicate with and work alongside our partners.

As a departure point, clearly, FWS biologists are noting and incorporating advancements in the conservation field. Progress remains patchy, however, as we often identify success with particular individuals or offices, rather than expecting it throughout the organization.

> We acknowledge the tremendous achievement of our biologists and managers over the past century. They have compiled a record of successful conservation actions and strategies that allow the FWS to proudly build on their work.

In answer to our charter, we recommend implementing Strategic Habitat Conservation as a defining characteristic of our bureau and our relationship with USGS. The question remains how shall we proceed? That is the nature of our report.

EXECUTIVE SUMMARY

The FWS has traditionally approached conservation with an emphasis on "more" - more protection, more restoration, and more management. We find opportunities in our programs, take action, and then report on completed projects using standard measurements, such as number of acres, river miles, and funds expended. Recent advances in the field of conservation science, however, are leading us in a new direction – a strategic pursuit of sustainable landscapes. These advances result from a growing body of information regarding conservation biology, landscape and population ecology, and adaptive resource management, along with improvements in remote sensing, database management, and geographic information systems (GIS). In short, activity based conservation with an emphasis on "more" gives way to the science of "how much more" and "where", as we consider how best to pursue our mission.

The change occurring across the conservation community includes a number of FWS offices and individual biologists. Our progress to date is promising, although patchy and inconsistent. In many cases, we lead the conservation community, while in others we simply seek to keep pace with partners and stakeholders. To take the next step, we need an organizational response that uses the principles of adaptive management. Our conservation actions for federal trust resources should increasingly flow from a cycle of 1) Biological Planning, 2) Conservation Design, 3) Conservation Delivery, and 4) Monitoring and Research. Using this framework, we improve our abilities to define desired biological outcomes and articulate the consequences of site-scale actions on landscape scale functions. We use the phrase *"strategic habitat conservation" (SHC)* to identify this iterative framework. Obviously, some trust resources face challenges that require consideration of factors other than habitat. All trust resources, however, need adequate habitat and SHC will help us address this challenge.

> **Overview of Recommendations**
>
> **Commit in principle** – senior leaders make a clear commitment that is visible in actions and on paper.
>
> **Expand understanding** - broaden employee understanding of Strategic Habitat Conservation
>
> **Expand engagement and ownership** – foster a commitment among employees to develop, implement, and use Strategic Habitat Conservation
>
> **Expand operational capacity** - increase and accelerate implementation of Strategic Habitat Conservation through adequate funding, training, outreach, evaluation, administrative services, and technological capabilities and functions.

The challenge of implementing SHC goes beyond the procedural. As a framework, SHC represents an approach, rather than a process or a new initiative. This framework will require an increased capacity for strategic Biological Planning, Conservation Design, and Monitoring and Research at ecoregional scales. Meeting this challenge will apply not only to the Service, but to our partner in science, USGS.

The proposal to adopt a more strategic approach to habitat conservation is timely given the current climate of lean budgets, increasing demands for accountability, and deteriorating conditions faced by many of our trust resources. SHC answers these challenges by offering efficiencies, better prioritization, and a strong, transparent basis for taking action. Further, working together on SHC will help the FWS and USGS enhance their relationship. The two bureaus can employ an improved conservation model that maximizes scientific, analytical, and administrative potential.

To encourage and expand the use of SHC, the following chapters address the change in our approach to conservation, including emerging methods, organizational capacity, and how best to recruit, prepare, and maintain an effective workforce. We recommend the FWS's Directorate and USGS's Executive Leadership Team take immediate steps to endorse and implement the SHC framework. By doing so, the FWS, with strong assistance from USGS, will become more efficient and effective at conserving priority habitats; will take actions that are increasingly based on scientific findings and adaptive management; and, ultimately, stakeholders and partners will find the bureaus more credible and accountable.

The nature of conservation has changed before and so has the FWS. Our biologists have already ensured a good start and we are confident that the FWS will not only keep pace with the change, but will continue to lend leadership and expertise in the future for management of the Nation's fish and wildlife resources.

CHAPTER ONE: The Changing Nature of Conservation

Introduction

The traditional U.S. Fish and Wildlife Service (FWS) conservation approach has frequently relied more on opportunity and less on scientific strategies. Resulting conservation priorities, policies, and actions have not fully benefited from landscape level considerations or the priorities and work of others. However, an increasing number of FWS offices, many in partnership with USGS, are moving the bureau in a different direction: one that features landscape level scientific analysis and coordinated on-the-ground actions. In many cases, these offices are leading the conservation community; and in others, FWS biologists are simply seeking to keep pace with partners and stakeholders. Chapter One characterizes changes in the field of conservation science and how the FWS and USGS can thrive.

The Catalysts of Change

- Advancements in conservation theory
- Geospatial technologies
- Increasing emphasis on accountability

Three catalysts are spurring change in the science and practice of conservation. As described below, these catalysts enable us to achieve conservation objectives more effectively and efficiently.

Advancements in Conservation Theory

To some extent, it is true that "all conservation is site-specific." But invariably, events at a broader scale (both in place and time) affect each conservation action. For example, we may manage habitat on a refuge in coastal Louisiana to increase duck populations, but the broader context of climate, hurricanes, and conditions on migration stopover and breeding habitat will surely affect our habitat management efforts. In turn, our site-specific actions can affect conservation efforts elsewhere. Recent advances in conservation theory seek to clarify the linkages between site-scale actions and processes at landscape, ecoregional, and continental scales. Knowledge of these linkages alters conservation objectives, strategies, and accompanying decisions.

Geospatial Technologies

Absent advancements in technology, a multi-scale approach to habitat conservation would remain essentially theoretical. Technological advancements in geospatial information management associated with remote sensing, GIS, and the Global Positioning System (GPS) allow theory to move to practice. Also, advances in GIS continue to improve our ability to support biological planning and assessment, along with inventory and monitoring at multiple scales.

Increasing Emphasis on Accountability

Increasing emphasis on accountability requires defensible methods of planning and transparently derived objectives and strategies. Accountability also requires an ability to deliver results based on realistic expectations. Very modest increases in conservation funding often come with an expectation of perceptible increases in fish and wildlife populations. When agencies do not have the ability to determine and communicate likely outcomes, they risk losing credibility. Accountability has become a defining feature of conservation, and successful agencies will need to articulate defensible scientific objectives.

The Science and Practice of Conservation

> • Goals/objectives emphasize biological outcomes
> • Models tie populations to landscape
> • Scientific findings inform management

The catalysts described above are leading to actual changes in the science and practice of conservation. These can be described in three broad categories.

Goals and Objectives Emphasize Biological Outcomes

Resource management has typically featured activities – protect, manage, restore – that serve as the overarching aim. Managers pursue opportunities with programmatic vigor, and the target is "more" – more protection, more restoration, and more management. An activity-based objective, such as pursuing more protection, management, or restoration, may lend itself to measurement and tracking. It does not, however, demand understanding of ecological conditions or rely on the scientific underpinnings of species-habitat interactions – because it does not define a measurable *end*.

> *"It is not enough to be busy. So are the ants. The question is 'What are we busy about?'"*
> Henry David Thoreau

Conversely, strategic habitat conservation (SHC) focuses on the ability of the landscape to sustain species as expressed in measurable objectives. Developing a strategy to attain a biological outcome, such as a population objective, requires documented and testable assumptions to determine whether the objective is met (Table 1). By using testable assumptions and evaluation of management outcomes, the aim to "protect, manage, and restore" finds value with specific, mission-based biological outcomes, rather than simply delivering "more".

Table 1. Comparison of Conservation Objectives for the Endangered Delmarva Fox Squirrel

Type of Objective	Objective	Characteristics of the Objective
Activity	"Increase level of forest management on the Eastern Neck NWR for Delmarva fox squirrels."	Does not require application of limiting factors, nor help prioritize research needs. Success could occur without benefiting the squirrels.
Biological Outcome	"Provide foraging habitat sufficient to sustain 1,000 Delmarva fox squirrels within the native forests of the Delmarva Peninsula."	Knowledge of limiting factors helps lead to "what, where, and how much" forest management sustains 1,000 squirrels. Provides basis for evaluating assumptions and monitoring success. Success relates to benefiting the squirrel population.

Models That Tie Populations to the Landscape

When knowledge of how ecosystems operate is incomplete, biological models are increasingly essential for synthesizing and applying current knowledge about species and habitats. Through models, biologists document uncertainties as testable assumptions, creating a direct link between management and research. Models also help describe the effect of habitat on populations and allow better access to empirical information or expert knowledge. When variables like land cover or elevation (spatial variables) are included, we can often better determine the unique potential of every site and landscape to contribute toward population objectives. Thus, we answer the questions "Where?" and "How much?" with more confidence. As a result, models that tie populations to habitats and management in a particular landscape provide the basis for setting transparent objectives. Finally, using results to help prioritize conservation actions and achieve objectives sets up an adaptive management loop – in other words, biologists can monitor conservation actions and use the results to inform future models and conservation actions.

Scientific Findings Inform Management
The relationship between research and management remains tenuous. As the conservation field continues to mature, however, researchers are trying to make their work more accessible to managers, and in turn, managers are increasingly turning to scientific findings. The SHC framework institutionalizes this relationship. The processes of building models, setting objectives based on biological outcomes, taking conservation actions, monitoring results, and changing actions as needed, requires the best available scientific knowledge and techniques. Further, as a manager undertakes this adaptive cycle, gaps in information and unfounded assumptions become apparent, leading to research priority setting for USGS and other partners.

Thriving Amidst Change
Biologists and managers are adjusting their approach to conserving species and habitats. The changes are systemic and founded on advances in science, technology, and accountability. They are here to stay. To thrive amidst these changes and improve our ability to conserve species and the ecological processes that sustain them, the FWS and USGS must take advantage of biological models, landscape level analyses, new technologies, biological models, and other emerging techniques and information resources. As premier agencies involved with the research and management of fish and wildlife resources, the FWS and USGS can embrace these changes and help provide leadership to the conservation community. SHC provides a framework that will allow us to lead coordinated, cooperative multi-partner habitat conservation efforts and build the capacity to conserve sustainable landscapes.

Introduction

SHC provides a framework for setting and achieving conservation objectives at multiple scales, based on the best available information, data, and ecological models. By applying this framework, we move away from opportunistic, program-specific activities to an approach that features a strategic focus.

Full implementation of SHC requires four elements that occur in an adaptive management loop: (1) Biological Planning, (2) Conservation Design, (3) Conservation Delivery, and (4) Monitoring and Research (Figure 1). Use of this framework answers vital questions about our conservation work - "How?", "Where?" and "How much?"

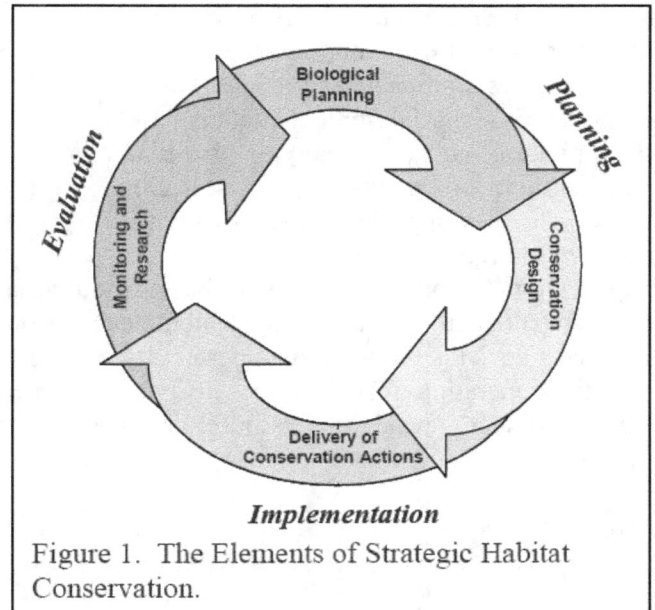

Figure 1. The Elements of Strategic Habitat Conservation.

No level of theory, planning, and design becomes meaningful until implemented. However, the framework for SHC becomes "strategic" because on-the-ground actions are based on planning and design and measured through monitoring and research. Through these strategies, habitat conservation can measurably benefit populations. The value of adaptive management, as an iterative process, has become widely recognized. SHC represents a form of adaptive management specifically tailored to habitat conservation.

Strategic Habitat Conservation – A Tool, Not a Rule

Even with increased cross-programmatic coordination, programs have varying statutory obligations, land bases, partnerships, budgetary limitations, staff capability and expertise. Consequently, SHC does not represent a prescriptive, one-size-fits-all approach. Rather, we present the SHC framework as a general guide to help us achieve our mission.

At the field level, SHC does not represent a turn to a prescriptive approach; rather biologists would still execute Program-specific responsibilities as the core of the third element - "Delivery of Conservation Actions." The Service and USGS, along with others, would build a capacity for Biological Planning and Conservation Design at ecoregional scales that support Programs and Field Stations in executing their duties strategically in a landscape context. The fourth element, "Monitoring and Research," would find relevance in the evaluation of assumptions and uncertainties inherent in Biological Planning and Conservation Design and would provide direction to existing and future monitoring efforts.

Each individual element of SHC has value, and partial use of the framework is generally preferable to ignoring the process entirely. However, the SHC framework achieves full value only when all four elements are effectively in place. Any resource management decision that occurs based on partial implementation should note limitations and accompanying assumptions and uncertainties. For example, conservation practitioners may apply Biological Planning, Conservation Design, and Delivery of the Conservation Action (Elements 1-3), but if resources are unavailable for Monitoring and Research (Element 4), future management decisions lose reliability. Nonetheless, a manager may face a decision with less than perfect information, but should do so recognizing uncertainty, rather than operating under false confidence. As the FWS implements SHC, using whatever data, expertise, time and other resources are available, the following principles of SHC are important to keep in mind:

> The NWRS will incorporate information derived from the SHC framework into the refuge planning process. This information will provide valuable assistance to refuge staffs and planners when evaluating and identifying the appropriate contribution that each refuge can make to larger landscape conservation priorities. Considered with NWRS mandates, policies, and guidance, the SHC framework will help facilitate development of wildlife and habitat management goals and objectives for comprehensive conservation plans (CCPs) and habitat management plans (HMPs) that will guide future management on over 540 refuges.

Guiding Principles

1. Habitat conservation is simply a means to attain our true goal – the conservation of populations and ecological functions that sustain them.
2. Defining measurable population objectives is a key component of SHC, at any scale.
3. Biological Planning must use the best scientific information available, both as a body of knowledge and a method of learning. Our understanding of ecological conditions is never perfect. An essential element of SHC is managing uncertainty through an iterative cycle of planning, doing, and evaluating.
4. Management actions, decisions, and recommendations must be defensible and transparent; thus, the implementation of SHC must be systematic, well documented, and explicit about the nature and magnitude of potential errors.
5. Conservation strategies consist of dynamic suites of objectives, tactics and tools that change as new information enters the SHC cycle.
6. Partnerships are essential, both for management and for developing conservation strategies.

In implementing SHC, the sixth guiding principle is especially important. Partnerships are a powerful means of communicating and implementing a conservation strategy. Whether a partnership focuses primarily on the conservation of Federal trust resources (e.g., migratory birds via joint ventures), or more broadly on the conservation of all fish and wildlife species in a particular ecoregion, partnerships allow us to integrate these priorities and decide who does what and where. Under this arrangement, each partner can fulfill its particular mandate, while working cooperatively. The priorities and actions developed from collaborating on the elements of SHC will also help partners realize when to work separately to achieve unique objectives. We realize the greatest impact of partnerships when partners jointly deliver and promote a common conservation strategy that achieves multiple objectives and respects the unique goals of each program.

Keeping the guiding principles in mind, Figure 2 depicts the SHC framework, with each element more fully described below. Please note that the elements of SHC, as well as associated sub-elements, may occur simultaneously and continuously, rather than in the sequential order of the text below. For example, monitoring and research may coincide with biological planning, or population objectives may occur after the current state of the system and limiting factors are identified. Finally, we may expand the concepts and principles of SHC to factors other than habitat.

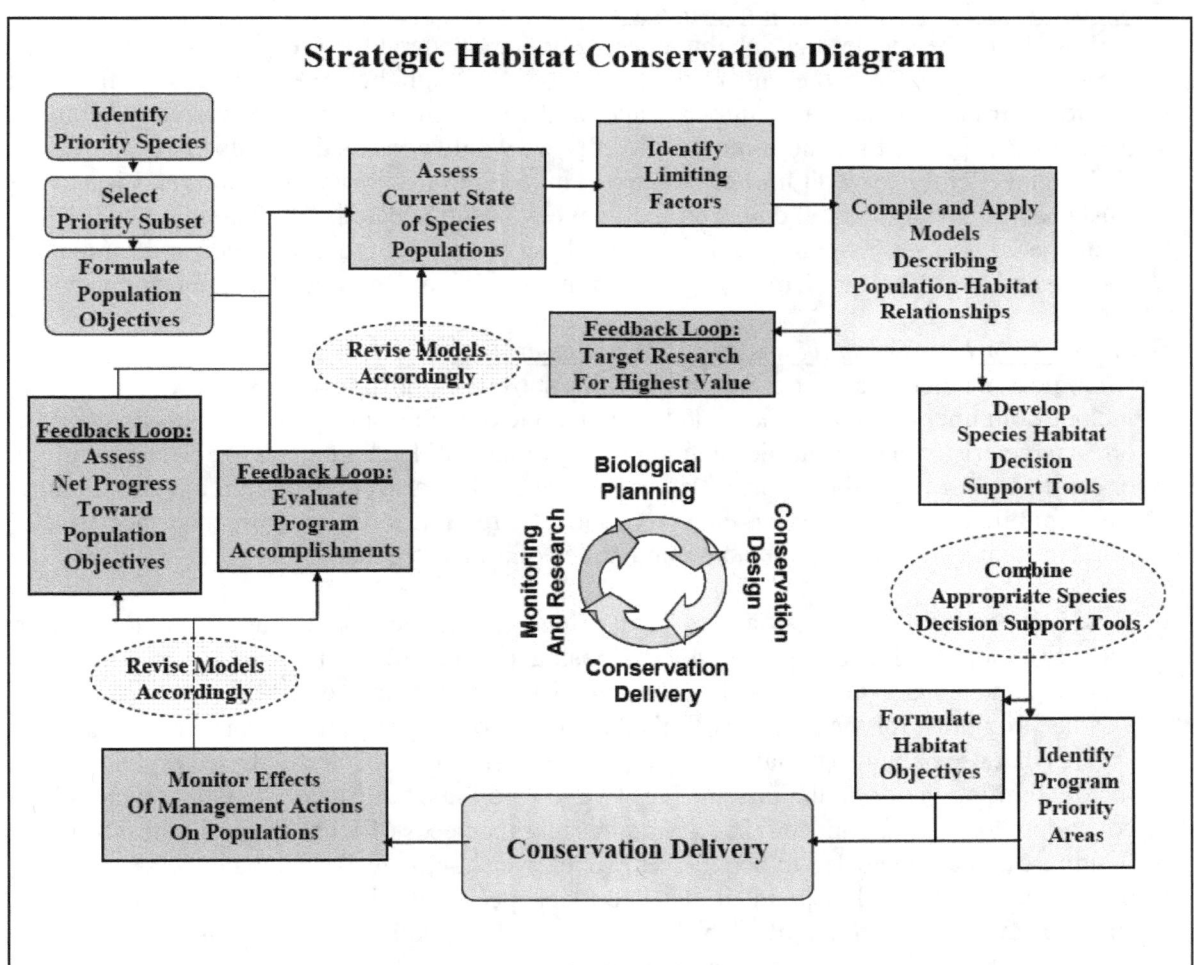

Figure 2. Schematic of the SHC framework at a landscape scale. Although depicted as a sequential process, some activities may occur simultaneously.

Element 1 – Biological Planning

- Identify priority species
- Select subset of priority species
- Formulate population objectives
- Assess current state of priority species
- Identify limiting factors
- Compile and apply models of population-habitat relationships

The Biological Planning element identifies clear goals and objectives and compiles information necessary to achieve them. Goals and objectives provide the motives for investing in a particular habitat or location. For the purposes of Biological Planning, a goal is a descriptive, open-ended, and often broad statement of desired future conditions that conveys purpose, but does not define measurable units. An objective elaborates on a goal. It provides a concise, measurable statement of what we want to achieve. The Biological Planning element, which consists of six sub-elements, ensures development of outcome-based objectives that flow from the best available data, information, and models.

Sub-element 1.1 – Identify Priority Species

Only some of the species that inhabit an ecoregion are Federal trust responsibilities, and, of these, a smaller subset represents priority species. Although the FWS seeks to benefit all species and to contribute to the health, integrity and biodiversity of ecosystems, we have an obligation to benefit trust species first and foremost. Ideally we would address the needs of all trust species with equal energy, but with limited resources, it becomes necessary to prioritize. Lists of priority trust species already exist and are routinely reviewed and updated. For example, the FWS Endangered Species Program maintains a database of endangered, threatened and candidate species and the Migratory Birds Program maintains a list of Birds of Management Concern.

Sub-element 1.2 – Select a Subset of Priority Species

Biological planners may choose to work with a subset of priority species. Selection criteria may include a number of legal, social, and biological factors, with some species sharing more than one characteristic. For example, statutory obligations will lead the FWS to select federally listed or candidate species to better prioritize actions, avoid jeopardy, and aid in recovery. In other cases, public demand and/or targeted programmatic funding may also influence species selection (e.g., providing fishable or huntable populations of a trust species).

In addition to legal and social factors influencing species selection, the use of *focal species* can provide a biologically sound method for choosing a subset of priority species to aid in Biological Planning and Conservation Design. Although the term may have different meanings among various programs, for the purpose of this document, focal species represent larger guilds of species that use habitats similarly. Generally, focal species are selected based on knowledge that factors limiting their populations are sensitive to landscape scale characteristics, such as land cover composition or connectivity. By addressing the needs of focal species, other trust species within a guild are expected to benefit. However, we should always evaluate the assumption that other species in a guild respond similarly to focal species. In the end, biologists must balance the specifics of their ecoregion, availability of data and information, and programmatic obligations to select an appropriate subset of priority species.

Sub-element 1.3 – Formulate Population Objectives

A population objective represents a measurable expression of a desired outcome. Population objectives are expressed as abundance, trend, vital rates, or other measurable indices of population status, and they are based on the best biological information about what constitutes a healthy population. Without population objectives there exists no basis for determining staff and funding resource needs for SHC, nor can we account for how efficiently these resources are used.

Sub-element 1.4 – Assess the Current State of Species Populations
If population objectives describe where we want to end up, the current state describes our starting point. If the current population occurs below the objective, the difference represents a conservation deficit. When habitat insufficiencies contribute to the conservation deficit, SHC aims to lay out and then follow an efficient route to make up the deficit at the lowest cost, consistent with other goals of FWS programs (e.g., public access). Obviously, to compare population objectives to the current state of populations, the two must have equivalent terms of reference. The models described in sub-element 1.6 may help assess the current state in terms of carrying capacity, recruitment, or survival rate.

Sub-element 1.5 – Identify Limiting Factors
Informed assumptions about the factors limiting populations or ecosystem function are critical to developing an efficient conservation strategy. To use a simple analogy, if an automobile manufacturer's output is limited by the number of tires their supplier can deliver, increasing the availability of transmissions will not have the desired impact. Because their goal is clear – the production of fully functioning automobiles – they will (1) work with their current supplier to increase tire output, or (2) find additional tire vendors.

> *"The presence and success of an organism or group of organisms depends upon a complex of conditions. Any condition which approaches or exceeds the limits of tolerance is said to be a limiting condition or a limiting factor...first and primary attention should be given to factors that are operationally significant to the organism at some time during its life cycle."* - Odum E.P. (1971) Fundamentals of Ecology

To use a biological example, low reproductive success resulting from nest predation and parasitism by edge species able to penetrate small forest patches may limit interior forest breeding birds. At an ecoregional scale, there are not enough large patches to sustain the population at desired levels of abundance. Birds that settle in small patches may fail to recruit young into the population, so individuals settling in large patches must maintain the population. Once we understand the factor limiting populations, several potential management treatments are possible:

- Use reforestation to create large patches
- Focus on increasing non-breeding survival
- Use predator and nest parasite control
- Raise the species in a hatchery and release

Generally, one or two management treatments will appear most practical and compatible with our goals for this ecosystem and other species that inhabit it. In this case, we would likely choose reforestation – coalescing small patches where recruitment is low into large patches where recruitment is higher. If survival remains the same and reproductive success increases in response to increasing patch size, the population will grow toward desired levels.

Mathematical expression of the relationship:

$$R = 0.419 + (0.847\sqrt{E})$$

Set of rules to express the relationship (heuristic):

Ratio of edge to area is greater than…	Ratio of edge to area is less than…	Recruitment Rate
0.00	0.02	0.10
0.02	0.04	0.21
0.04	0.06	0.50
0.06	0.08	0.66
0.08	0.12	0.75
0.12	0.20	0.82
0.20	0.30	0.85
0.3		0.90

Graphical expression of the relationship:

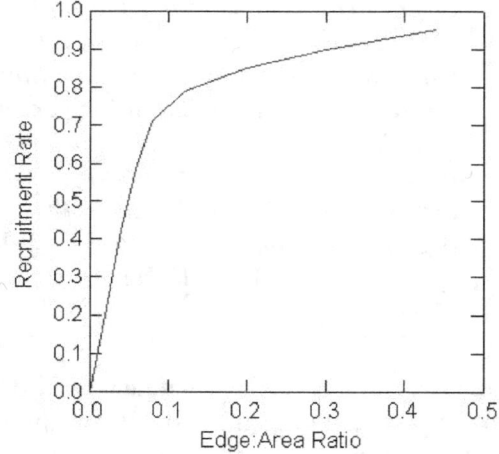

Figure 3. Three expressions of a model that relates the rate of bird recruitment (R) to the ratio of forest edge length to patch area (E).

Next, we begin to answer the interrelated questions of *how much* management and *where*? We ultimately answer these questions through Conservation Design (element 2 of SHC). Initiating Conservation Design, however, requires an understanding of the relationship between populations and habitats. Models are useful descriptions of what we know or assume about how a population responds to habitat – particularly the factors limiting the potential of the habitat to sustain selected species. We use models to assess the current state of the ecosystem in terms of its ability to support populations, and to determine how best to make up the population deficit and attain our desired objective.

Staying with our forest breeding bird example, we learn from available data that the ratio of patch edge to area limits recruitment rate – as patches become larger and blockier, recruitment rate increases. As a result, answering the questions of *where* and *how much* requires models that describe the relationship between the edge to area ratio and recruitment rate. Figure 3 illustrates several means of describing this hypothetical relationship. We see that after the edge to area ratio exceeds 0.1 (about 120 acres for a square patch, larger for irregularly shaped patches), further increases in recruitment rate start to slow down. We have reached the point of diminishing returns. A strategic approach to attaining our habitat objectives would indicate that once we have reached a ratio of 0.1, we should move on to a new area rather than continue to make the same patch bigger and bigger for less and less additional benefit.

Whether based on data or expert opinion, the use of models serves as a defining feature of SHC. Models help us describe in measurable terms what we know or assume about the probable response of a population to habitat and how our actions provide an effect.

Why model at an ecoregional scale?

The relationship of species to their habitats varies among regions of the U.S. Species use different habitats for different purposes at different relative densities. An effective conservation strategy for forest breeding birds in the southeastern U.S. may not work for the Pacific Northwest. Thus, building an effective and efficient conservation strategy requires a geographic approach within which species of concern, habitat types, habitat use, threats to habitats, and habitat potential are relatively homogeneous. This enables the use of models and a systematic application of the biological foundation.

Without models, it remains difficult to systematically apply the biological foundation for management.

Element 2 – Conservation Design

- Develop species habitat decision support tools
- Designate priority areas
- Formulate habitat objectives

Conservation Design brings together the results of Biological Planning into one or a few products that are accessible to diverse stakeholders. The most common products of Conservation Design are maps. Maps can be extremely compelling, but beware: a map is no more accurate than the information that went into creating it. Conservation Design, which consists of three sub-elements, provides the on-the-ground strategy for achieving objectives.

Sub-element 2.1 – Develop Species Habitat Decision Support Tools
A decision support tool combines geospatial data, biological information, and the results of ecological models into a format that helps managers decide which conservation actions to apply to a given landscape (Fig. 4). Decision support tools should be linked to specific treatments that target a population response. The decision support tool arranges available information relevant to the decision into a single format, allowing the manager to view the compilation of the data, information, and models in a simple form.

Decision support tools provide a way to evaluate the potential of every acre of habitat to support desired populations of a species by summarizing, at a glance, available information regarding accompanying habitat types. These tools may also be developed for ecological functions like water quality enhancement, flood damage reduction, or carbon sequestration. The FWS and USGS may choose to invest in developing these or other types of decision support tools in order to further the conservation of Federal trust species by broadening the appeal of our strategies and the diversity of our partnerships. Decision support tools can be used individually or in combinations to direct activities or advise partner programs. However, as the phrase indicates, these are tools meant to support a decision, not supplant the decision maker.

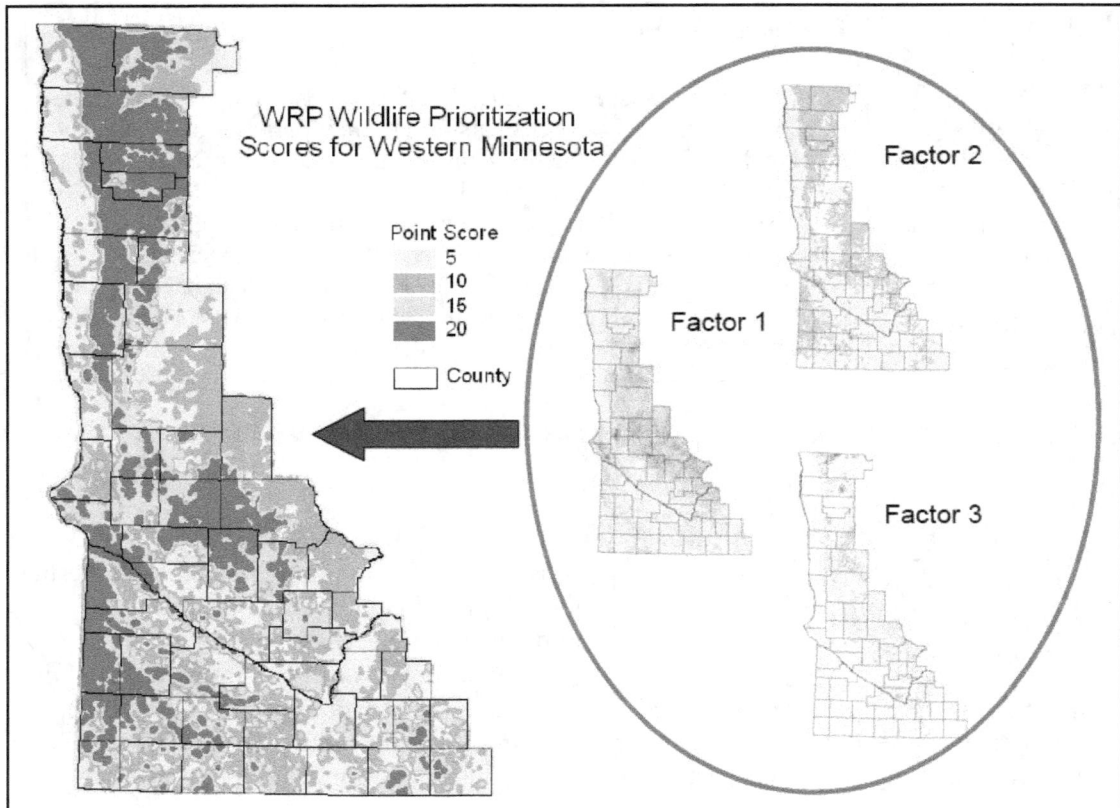

Figure 4. Example of programmatic application of decision support tools. When the USDA-NRCS expressed an interest in supporting migratory bird goals through the Wetland Reserve Program (WRP), the FWS helped them target priority areas in western Minnesota. Having a portfolio of species habitat decision support tools that were appropriate to this program (represented by Factors 1-3) made assistance quick and effective. More than $15 million/year of USDA funding in Minnesota is contributing to the strategic conservation of migratory bird populations.

Sub-element 2.2 – Designate Priority Areas

Most of the time, decisions about where to protect or restore a particular habitat type or where to deliver a particular program are based on the potential of each landscape to provide desired benefits. Desired benefits might be as narrowly defined as the potential to support multiple species of ducks (as in the FWS's Waterfowl Production Area program), to as broadly defined as wildlife, clean water, and soil retention (as in USDA's Wetland Reserve Program).

When we combine priorities identified by decision support tools for multiple species that occupy the same area and can benefit from a particular conservation action, the product is a depiction of where aggregate benefits can occur for Federal trust species. These kinds of priority areas may be useful throughout the FWS, ranging from land acquisition by the NWRS, to priorities for

Partners for Fish and Wildlife projects, or as decision tools that assist Ecological Services staff with environmental reviews.

The systematic evaluation of species and habitat conservation strategies provide for decision-making in a more structured, scientific manner to better accommodate the needs of trust resources. When "spatially-explicit" conservation strategies are developed by applying models to geospatial data, managers can operate in an awareness of the conservation needs and strategies for multiple species and guilds, as well as other ecological functions. Thus, managers may seek opportunities to leverage benefits for one species with another, estimate their accomplishments and the impacts of partners on the attainment of their objectives, and anticipate and pro-actively address potential conflicting responses of species to habitat management.

The Habitat and Population Evaluation Team (HAPET) of the Prairie Potholes Joint Venture had developed landscape level models for ruddy ducks. They used these models to develop a decision support tool to estimate a habitat objective necessary to mitigate a number of ruddy duck deaths attributable to an oil spill in the Chesapeake Bay. The information was used to direct the expenditure of $600K to restore ruddy duck breeding habitat. HAPET's rapid response ensured that the funding was directed toward the restoration of habitat where it would most likely mitigate duck losses.

Sub-element 2.3 – Formulate Habitat Objectives
Models and priority areas can help estimate the amount of habitat of each type required to attain population objectives. This information enables us to establish habitat objectives that directly relate to achieving our population objectives. Relative conservation efficiency (e.g., biological benefits/acre) varies across landscapes. Thus, the actual amount of habitat required to attain our population objectives depends on where we deliver our programs. Nonetheless, even crudely estimated habitat objectives enable us to convey the magnitude of required conservation actions to partners and stakeholders. Timely adjustments to habitat objectives may be made based on new scientific information, recent management accomplishments, and other influences on habitat due to policy changes and socioeconomic factors. The same process used to set habitat objectives may also be used to predict population impacts of these policy and socioeconomic factors.

Element 3 – Conservation Delivery
SHC represents a framework for compiling, interpreting and refining the biological foundation for trust resource conservation. It provides for day-to-day use of scientific information to guide an array of management decisions regarding how and where to efficiently attain trust resource conservation objectives. As an integral part of SHC, "Delivery of Conservation Actions" will be the subject of a considerable amount of future discussion, including the changing role of the Service in collaborative conservation. The first steps are to understand our role in partnerships as the lead agency for trust resource conservation and to create an internal and external expectation that the Service and USGS will strive for a more strategic and efficient approach with our own contribution to conservation delivery. Whereas the Service has a considerable capacity for conservation delivery, the NEAT has focused primarily on building the largely heretofore undeveloped capacity for biological planning, conservation design and targeted research and monitoring.

In the future, the Service will be equally a manager of populations and habitats <u>and</u> the steward and purveyor of the biological foundation for Federal trust species conservation. The latter function has significant implications for how the Service operates with others. Partnerships are valuable to the extent that they enable conservation that exceeds the sum of the potential actions of the individual agencies and organizations that comprise them. Among traditional conservation delivery functions, future conservation partnerships will function as a nexus for information between the scientific community and the agencies and programs seeking diverse natural resource enhancement benefits through habitat conservation. In many cases, more diverse partnerships will eventually be needed to bring together expertise on economics, sociology, hydrology, as well as biology, for the purpose of developing a comprehensive land use strategies that enable humans and wildlife to co-exist at objective levels of abundance. No one should purport to understand the details of how partnerships like these will function most effectively; however, SHC is an open-ended framework that enables integration of any environmental or socio-economic factors that can be measured and predicted based on landscape context.

Implementation of on-the-ground actions based on information from Biological Planning and Conservation Design (SHC elements one and two) results in the application of specific conservation actions on specific parts of the landscape. Managers constantly make decisions about what conservation treatments to apply and where to apply them. The framework of SHC offers managers access to a variety of tools developed from the best available data and information to make those decisions. They will have transparent and defensible reasons for applying treatments. Finally, they will have targeted research and monitoring to validate or help them adjust their management decisions.

Element 4 – Monitoring and Research

• Target research for value to resource management
• Establish monitoring activities to support inferences
• Use monitoring and research in a feedback loop.

Monitoring and Research are a prominent and fundamental element of SHC, and without this step, we lose the iterative process whereby managers learn and increase their efficiency. The FWS cannot afford to undertake large scale habitat protection, restoration or enhancement endeavors, only to discover after years of management that actions were ineffective or even counterproductive. Monitoring and Research, which consists of three sub-elements, helps evaluate:

- assumptions made in population-habitat models and decision support tools;
- habitat responses to conservation actions;
- population responses to conservation actions; and
- progress toward habitat and population objectives.

Sub-element 4.1 – Target Research to Provide the Highest Value to Resource Management
Implementation of the first three elements of SHC (Biological Planning, Conservation Design, and Conservation Delivery) reveals uncertainties in the biological foundation we use for management. In the absence of perfect knowledge, biologists are forced to make assumptions, but they can treat these assumptions as testable hypotheses. Research provides the avenue for conducting the tests and supporting or disproving the hypotheses. Not all assumptions, however,

are equally important. Those assumptions having the greatest impact on management decisions are the highest priorities for research.

Identifying research priorities using SHC will help the FWS target research at mission critical information. With research priorities in hand, the FWS can collaborate more effectively with USGS and the rest of the research community. As a systematic use of the biological foundation, both as a means of learning and as a growing body of knowledge, SHC helps bridge the gap between managers and researchers.

Sub-element 4.2 – Establish Monitoring Activities to Support Inferences
When applying management actions to a given site, the FWS infers which habitat management actions will produce the most efficient effect on populations. To evaluate whether management actions are having the predicted consequences, we need to monitor actual outcomes, most often using a representative sample of sites to ensure that, on average, the effects of a particular type of treatment match expectations. Such effects, when tallied up over larger areas, or for an entire region, enable us to infer a program's effectiveness. We then revise and refine our predictions so that future iterations of our conservation strategy are more reliable.

Sub-element 4.3 – Use Monitoring and Research in a Feedback Loop
New information from research and monitoring only becomes useful if it influences future conservation decisions and actions. These benefits are most pronounced when the elements of SHC are iterative and ongoing rather than static or episodic. Thus, habitat conservation strategies are most appropriately viewed as *living* strategies that are continually developing in response to targeted research and inferential monitoring data.

All elements of SHC are part of a continuous feedback loop. In fact, successful application of any element of SHC depends upon awareness of the information being developed in other elements. Nonetheless, we highlight the critical importance of Monitoring and Research because, all too often, information from this element is implicitly viewed as the end of the process, rather than an indispensable part of a cycle.

CHAPTER THREE: Building Joint Capability for the FWS and USGS

A Direction for Change

The SHC Framework presents both FWS and USGS with significant challenges. The four functional elements will require a more complex science/management relationship – one that treats science not simply as what we know, but how we operate. In recommending SHC as the Service's conservation framework, we do not propose that the Service duplicate the Survey's science capabilities. Rather, we recommend the Service operate within a conservation framework that increases both the demand for and relevance of USGS science. For the Service, SHC means increasing our capability for biological planning and conservation design at broad spatial scales. For USGS, SHC represents a recognition that the Service's science needs will increasingly extend beyond traditional research.

The FWS has long operated as a science-based organization and our conservation actions are rooted in a broad body of scientific knowledge that USGS has helped develop. Yet, as the Service embraces SHC, our science needs will extend to predictive modeling, landscape characterization, decision-based monitoring, and assumption-driven research. Fortunately, all USGS science disciplines are recognizing the need to not simply grow the body of knowledge through basic research, but to predict, monitor, and assess ecological change within an interdisciplinary context. We see SHC as the framework for merging the increasingly complex needs of both organizations. In the future, we will require that FWS and USGS work collaboratively to:

1. Develop an integrated capacity for Biological Planning and Conservation Design at ecoregional scales (see Appendix C - Technical Skills and Infrastructure Needs);
2. Create ecoregional partnerships focused on leveraging the resources of the conservation community; and
3. Reengineer decision-making processes to link Biological Planning, Conservation Design, Conservation Delivery, and Monitoring and Research iteratively in an adaptive cycle of science.

A number of FWS field offices employ collaborative conservation efforts, driven by partnerships and conducted within the framework of SHC. The FWS needs to learn from those efforts and expand on them to build a stronger, more comprehensive partnership with USGS.

Strengthening Institutional Relationships

Although the Service's science partners extend beyond USGS, we cannot overstate the importance of a strong institutional relationship between FWS and USGS in advancing the SHC framework. While our missions are distinct, our federal trust responsibilities are intertwined. We should remember that past organizational changes, though they served to separate us administratively, were undertaken with the intent of strengthening the science/management relationship within the Department of the Interior. The SHC framework provides an opportunity to progress with this intent.

We have previously noted the progress of FWS field stations in responding to the changing nature of conservation. Progress to date depends on a close, if not dynamic FWS/USGS relationship, built on the strength of interpersonal relationships. Yet each time offices and individuals reach across agency lines in a context other than research needs/response, they must begin by redefining their own inter-office level roles, relationships, and responsibilities. Doing so is not a trivial exercise. We challenge the Directorate of both agencies to support emerging cross bureau work with the power of institutional relationships redefined to support the functional elements of SHC. Appendix B provides a draft Memorandum of Understanding intended to facilitate and support the integrated relationship that SHC requires. Again, we see a new future – one in which FWS conservation biologists are supported by USGS scientists in a unified conservation framework of biological planning, conservation design, conservation delivery, decision-based monitoring, and assumption-driven research.

Strengthening Operational Relationships

* Biological Planning
* Conservation Design
* Conservation Delivery
* Research and Monitoring

To the extent that the FWS embraces SHC, we will require a partnership with USGS that effectively addresses *each* of the four functional elements described in Chapter 2: Biological Planning, Conservation Design, Delivery of Conservation Actions, and Research and Monitoring. In effective partnerships, capabilities complement one another. Roles emanate from the different functions of the bureaus – one, a management agency charged with the conservation of populations, and the other, a research agency charged with providing scientific information and conducting scholarly research suitable for publication in peer reviewed journals. The respective roles help establish who should do what in each of the four elements of SHC.

Biological Planning – As a key management agency responsible for Federal trust resource conservation, via environmental statutes, the FWS identifies priority species and works with stakeholders to determine population objectives. Scientists within both bureaus and from other partner agencies determine potential limiting factors and compile models. USGS will typically contribute to the completion of technical models, with the methods and results suitable for journal publication.

Conservation Design – The FWS will often serve as a lead for spatial analysis and use of models and GIS technology to designate priority areas for federal trust species, but partners and stakeholders will also have roles to play. In particular, our partnership with USGS will increase the FWS capacity to accomplish this type of work in areas lacking sufficient staff or expertise. In addition, USGS will continue to develop and distribute many required spatial data layers, such as land cover, elevation, etc. It remains vital that USGS consult with FWS end users of spatial data before and during data development to ensure that spatial resolution and classification systems are suitable for the FWS's conservation design needs.

We do not anticipate that every FWS Administrative Region would use the same geographic framework for SHC. Each approach, however, should have:

* Geographic units that are relatively ecologically homogeneous (i.e., contain a single ecosystem type to facilitate Biological Planning and to aid in making inferences from Research and Monitoring);

- Geographic unit definition is spatially comprehensive (i.e., boundary definitions encompass entire country without overlap).
- A manageable number of geographic units – neither too many nor too few (and therefore too heterogeneous);

Ecological regions do not follow political boundaries, although some use of political boundaries may occur for pragmatic reasons. Defining the appropriate geographic framework is another part of Conservation Design where FWS and USGS will need to work closely, and with partners and stakeholders.

Conservation Delivery – Clearly, implementation of habitat conservation is the role of the FWS. However, planning, design, evaluation and implementation, the tenets of SHC are all linked in a continuous iterative process. A constant dialog between managers, planners, and researchers is essential to the process. SHC, therefore, provides a venue within which USGS science and information can influence where and how management occurs.

Research and Monitoring – A USGS contribution to research and monitoring is indispensable, but the FWS and USGS both have a role in ensuring that research results affect future management. In Chapter 2 we state that monitoring and research must be carried out to evaluate:
- assumptions made in population-habitat models and decision support tools;
- habitat responses to conservation actions;
- population responses to conservation actions; and
- progress toward habitat and population objectives.

The first bullet is research targeted at FWS assumptions identified through the Biological Planning element. Whereas FWS staff must articulate these assumptions and related research needs, it will generally fall to USGS and other scientists to conduct the research – develop the methods, collect, analyze and interpret data, and publish results.

The other bullets represent monitoring. Site-scale monitoring of habitat and population response to management should be performed by FWS field staff as a routine management function. USGS may assist with monitoring design and data analysis as needed. Ecoregional and national scale monitoring of Federal trust species population and habitat status and trends are logically the responsibility of the FWS as an agency legally mandated to ensure their conservation. There is, however, a clear supporting role for USGS in survey design, data management, and analysis, and there may be roles for other partners as well.

CHAPTER FOUR: Recommendations

Introduction

We have developed an ambitious set of recommendations to formulate, embrace and support SHC. We offer our recommendations to assist the FWS's Directorate and USGS's Executive Leadership Team in:

1. Articulating a new and shared conservation approach via SHC; and

2. Leading a gradual and progressive effort to embrace, implement and support the new conservation framework and use it to guide agency planning, priorities, and decisions.

Recommendations are made with the understanding that other efforts are currently underway that seek change. With budget challenges, increasing breadth and volume of workload, and a changing workforce, our bureaus face a unique opportunity to prepare for the next decade and beyond. Venues like the "Shaping Our Future" Workshop and initiatives such as "Future Challenges" are just a few endeavors that complement policy deliberations and decisions that seek increased efficiencies and effectiveness through cross-programmatic delivery of our mission.

The recommendations are organized under four headings that reflect complementary aspects of expanding SHC capacity. Also, we have not identified all the actions that the two bureaus could or should undertake.

> **Overview of Recommendations**
>
> **Commit in principle** – senior leaders make a clear commitment that is visible in actions and on paper.
>
> **Expand understanding** - broaden employee understanding of Strategic Habitat Conservation.
>
> **Expand engagement and ownership** – foster a commitment among employees to develop, implement, and use Strategic Habitat Conservation.
>
> **Expand operational capacity** - increase and accelerate implementation of Strategic Habitat Conservation through adequate funding, training, outreach, evaluation, administrative services, and technological capabilities and functions.

As we receive feedback from Directorate members, bureau employees, and our partners, recommendations and actions will evolve.

We also assign a recommended time frame for performing each action item as **Immediate (0-2 years)**, meaning items that need to occur without delay to capture existing momentum within our bureaus; **Near-term (2-5 years)**, referring to minimal or relatively low-cost actions that will take longer to initiate but are critical to foster change; and (3) **Long-term (5 years +)**, representing actions requiring a significant accretion or potential redirection of resources to accomplish, but that are ultimately the full manifestation of a FWS-USGS partnership that uses the SHC framework.

Finally, developing and implementing these recommendations will require a considerable investment of time by a dedicated team of FWS and USGS staff. We suggest creation of a national implementation task force to facilitate a FWS and USGS-wide dialog on SHC concepts, various manifestations of current species lists and their use, and to ensure consideration and implementation of our recommendations, as appropriate.

Recommended Actions
Commit in Principle

1.1 The Service Directorate and USGS Executive Leadership Team endorse SHC as a shared conservation framework (Immediate).

1.2 The Service Directorate and USGS Executive Leadership Team promote refining, strengthening, and expanding science/management relationships between the organizations by entering into a Memorandum of Understanding that guides the establishment of operational relationships and procedures. (see Appendix B for a draft MOU) (Immediate).

1.3 Establish a National Implementation Task Force (NITF)

1.4 Develop a fiscal year 2008 budget approach to begin implementing capacity building measures for SHC (Immediate).

Expand Understanding

2.1 Facilitate national outreach on SHC concepts and methods via the NITF to:
> 2.1.1 Conduct inreach and outreach on SHC concepts, methods, and recommendations (Immediate).
> 2.1.2 Share concepts with FWS and USGS staff (Immediate).
> 2.1.3 Complete and make available a practitioner's handbook (Immediate).

2.2 Conduct a national workshop for regional and program leaders to increase knowledge on SHC concepts and methods and obtain staff feedback on specific needs to implement SHC (Immediate).

2.3 Conduct regional workshops for a wider, cross-program audience for field managers and biologists (these could be through distance learning followed by on-line communication tools) (Immediate).

2.4 Brief bureau, DOI and OMB staff involved with budget construction/oversight, accountability reporting via GPRA, DOI Strategic Plan, PART review process, etc., and stakeholder outreach (Immediate).

2.5 Develop curricula (accessing current FWS/USGS practitioners) and institute new NCTC training that address SHC concepts by:
> 2.5.1 Assigning technical staff specializing in Biological Planning and Conservation Design to provide detailed information on model development, application, monitoring design, etc. (Near-term).

2.5.2 Informing project leaders and other program staff (end users of assessment products) on basic approaches and applications of SHC (Near-term).

2.6 Initiate a partnership strategy to:
    2.6.1 Share SHC concepts with states and solicit input (Immediate).
    2.6.2 Review State Comprehensive Wildlife Management Strategies and identify opportunities to develop cooperative capacity for SHC (Immediate).
    2.6.3 Establish a "community of practice" whereby the FWS convenes members of the conservation community to share methods and approaches for SHC (Near-term).

2.7 Identify cross-programmatic teams to help provide outreach and training (Immediate).

Expand Engagement and Ownership

3.1 Develop and implement performance standards and program objectives relating to SHC:
    3.1.1 Create program objectives based on full implementation of SHC (Long-term).
    3.1.2 Add performance standards based on SHC concepts to the Employee Performance Appraisal Plans of pertinent resource management program supervisors and employees (Near-term).
    3.1.3 Create program objectives and performance standards to build partnerships for sharing in the implementation of SHC (Near-term).

3.2 Develop national and regional cooperative agreements based on the MOU between FWS and USGS to integrate staff and resources and build capacity for SHC (Near-term).

3.3 Include NIFT members in workforce planning sessions and efforts, in addition to other strategic initiatives, including the Decision Analysis Community of Practice, Science Committee, Information Quality group, Future Challenges, etc. (Near-term).

3.4 Seek better integration of programmatic conservation priorities and develop protocols for making structured, strategic decisions where priorities are potentially in conflict. (Near-term).

Expand Operational Capacity

4.1 Analyze current abilities to conduct the Biological Planning and Conservation Design elements of SHC:
    4.1.1 Review Biological Planning and Conservation Design assets within FWS and USGS administrative regions and ecological regions (Immediate).
    4.1.2 Analyze current status and capability for providing land cover data, National Wetland Inventory data, and other digital data layers for SHC efforts (Immediate).
    4.1.3 Develop regional strategies for building capacity (Near-term).

4.2 Build SHC capacity by:
    4.2.1 Augmenting current conservation assessment efforts already underway in priority ecological regions (e.g., joint venture offices, Refuge Goals Coordinators, USGS, etc.) by
        4.2.1.1 Sharing programmatic assets for biological planning and conservation design (Near-term);

4.2.1.2 Consolidating existing programmatic staff into cross-program teams (Near-term); and

4.2.2 Establishing capacity in other ecological regions that are high priorities for the FWS (Near-term).

4.3 Implement geospatial data and technology recommendations (see Appendix E).

4.3.1: Establish national and ecoregional inter-bureau teams to identify and prioritize base data needs to facilitate SHC and support cost-effective, collaborative data acquisition efforts (Near-term).

4.3.2: Establish national and ecoregional inter-bureau teams to ensure that data conform to required standards, are relevant to the region(s) that collect them, and facilitate cross-regional coordination on SHC (Near-term).

4.3.3 Provide mechanism for developing, documenting, and sharing common GIS tools and models (Near-term).

4.3.4 Identify hardware, bandwidth, and other technical infrastructure requirements at strategic locations, such as Joint Venture offices and co-located field offices (Near-term).

4.3.5 Identify topics for joint training opportunities, such as metadata, advanced GIS applications, and advanced software technical support (Near-term).

4.4 Conduct an inter-bureau review of administrative procedures that hinder cooperation between the FWS, USGS and other DOI bureaus, and recommend appropriate resolutions (Immediate).

4.5 As new endangered and threatened species recovery plans are developed and older ones are revised, ensure that the species' status assessments and habitat goals and criteria are framed, to the extent possible, in terms that lend themselves to integration within the SHC framework. The same concept should be applied to the development of candidate conservation programs. (mid-term to long-term).

4.6 Develop an apprentice/internship program that provides learning opportunities for bureau biologists and scientists conducting SHC. Existing teams (reference 4.2.1) may serve as locations:

4.7.1 Establish 30-60 day details (Immediate).

4.7.2 Establish 1-2 year internships (Near-term). (Appendix D)

4.7.3 Arrange job swaps between FWS and USGS staff with compatible background and skills (Near-term).

4.8 Secure increased annual program funding to hire monitoring staff who collect biological information to evaluate consequences of management actions and assumptions (Long-term).

4.9 Establish protocols for accomplishment reporting in terms of biological impacts as well as acres effected and dollars expended (Near-term).

4.10 Implement an approach to allocate funds based on accomplishments and efficiencies of a region or station to achieve biological objectives that arise from SHC (Near-term).

4.11 Secure reliable increased annual funding for targeted research (Long-term).

GLOSSARY

Decision support tool (DST): Maps, data bases and other tools built from geospatial data, biological information, and the results of ecological models that help a manager decide which conservation actions to apply to a given landscape.

Focal species: A species used for conservation assessment, especially a species that represents a guild or larger group of species that use habitat similarly. The use of focal species is a planning shortcut when collecting data or building models for priority species.

Geospatial: Relating to data, services, databases or other items that are geographically referenced and thus can be linked to a location on the earth (sometimes abbreviated to spatial).

Limiting factor: A primary factor constraining the growth of a population toward objective levels.

Strategic Habitat Conservation (SHC): A framework for setting and achieving conservation objectives at multiple scales based on the best available information, data, and ecological models. Full implementation of SHC requires four elements that occur in an adaptive management loop: (1) biological planning, (2) conservation design, (3) delivery of conservation actions, and (4) monitoring and research.

APPENDIX A

U.S. Fish & Wildlife Service and U.S. Geological Survey
National Ecological Assessment Team
CHARTER

Purpose	Several FWS initiatives focus on developing nation-wide, science-based conservation strategies. The USGS is focusing on integrating science and information in geographic regions to support multiple conservation and management needs. The National Ecological Assessment Team will integrate these efforts into a consistent Service-wide approach to setting and prioritizing conservation goals for trust species, important habitats, and other conservation targets.
	This approach will focus will enable development of habitat conservation strategies at the ecosystem level and will support adaptive management. The approach will be based on use of the best available information on factors limiting populations and ecological integrity. Finally, this approach will serve as the foundation for cross-program coordination of conservation activities within the Service, as well as joint conservation ventures with our partners.
The Team is empowered	1) to design a cross-programmatic approach to science-based ecological assessment for the Service; 2) to recommend a unified implementation structure and process, including guidance on the implementation roles and responsibilities of each program; and 3) to use the resources of their respective offices, to travel, and to request and receive assistance of other offices as necessary to achieve their purpose.
Participants	The Team consists of representatives from 5 FWS program areas: Refuges, Migratory Birds-State Programs, Endangered Species, Fisheries, and Habitat Conservation. Team members will include staff involved in the Refuge System's "Habitat Goals" process, the Migratory Birds/Joint Venture science teams, and others with an appropriate background in science-based conservation planning. The team also includes representation from the biological and information disciplines of the U.S. Geological Survey, who will coordinate needs across USGS.
Process	The team will 1) develop a time line with a detailed schedule for product delivery, including internal and external review periods; 2) assess and integrate relevant ecological assessment methods and other documents, including Joint Venture initiatives, the NWRS final report for integrating habitat goals and objectives for conservation, and sound science-based ecosystem team approaches; 3) consider other appropriate ecological assessment concepts and approaches used by States and other outside organizations; and 4) prepare a report and recommendations for the Directorates of both bureaus

Products and Services

- Refine and merge the individual program strategies into an integrated Service-wide approach.
- Identify work force needs, roles and responsibilities of each program in supporting implementation.
- Identify priority science and information systems to be developed in partnership with USGS and others.
- Analyze alternative, phased implementation strategies and corresponding budget

recommendations, including an alternative involving the realignment of existing budget and personnel; recommend a preferred alternative.

- Recommend a geographic framework and associated information infrastructure for seamless, nationwide application of ecological assessment.

Reporting Relationships

The team will be chartered by the Directors of the Fish & Wildlife Service and the Geological Survey and reports to the Directorate Oversight Council (FWS Assistant Directors for MBSP and NWRS, FWS Regional Directors from regions 1, 3, 4, and 5, FWS Science Advisor to the Director, FWS Special Assistant to the Director, USGS Associate Director for Biology, and USGS Geographic Information Officer). The FWS Science Advisor will serve as the Directorate Oversight Council's primary liaison to the National Ecological Assessment Team.

APPENDIX B

MEMORANDUM OF UNDERSTANDING

Between the U.S. Fish and Wildlife Service and U.S. Geologic Survey

ON STRENGTHENING THE SCIENCE/MANAGEMENT RELATIONSHIP
IN THE CONSERVATION OF FISH AND WILDLIFE RESOURCES

PURPOSE

The purpose of this Memorandum of Understanding (MOU) is broadly one of refining, strengthening, and expanding the science/management relationship between the U.S. Fish and Wildlife Service (hereafter FWS or Service) and the U.S. Geologic Survey (hereafter USGS or Survey) in exercising the federal trust for fish and wildlife conservation. More specifically, the purpose is to facilitate development of (eco)regional agreements between the Service and USGS that will support both agencies in attaining their goals by promoting collaborative relationships within a unified conservation framework.

BACKGROUND

Advances in conservation theory and information management technologies are merging with increasing demands for organizational accountability to change the nature of conservation. Increasingly, both the problems and the solutions of natural resource management are being seen in a multi-scaled, interdisciplinary context. The conservation strategies of resource agencies such as the Service are expected to be spatially explicit in orientation, multi-scaled in approach, adaptive in delivery, and outcome driven in results. Likewise, the role of USGS as an interagency science resource is increasingly seen as extending beyond research to one of predicting, monitoring, and assessing ecological change in an interdisciplinary context. The changing nature of conservation both anticipates and requires a more complex and robust relationship between science and management.

As a response to these challenges, an interagency team of FWS and USGS biologists have put forth and the Service Directorate has adopted a unifying framework of biological planning, conservation design, conservation delivery, decision-based monitoring, and assumption-driven research that is termed "strategic habitat conservation" (SHC). As the Service embraces this conservation framework, its science support needs will become functionally more complex; and it will have need to expand its capacity for population/habitat modeling, landscape characterization and assessment, integrated monitoring, and biological information management at ecoregional scales. The growing capabilities of USGS in the areas will become ever more critical and relevant to the Service's operational success. Accordingly, the functional elements of SHC should be viewed as a unifying framework in which both organizations work collaboratively to create a more operationally effective Service-USGS relationship – one that has both agencies working less in a customer/client relationship and more as partners with common goals, a shared sense of purpose, and working within a defined framework of strategic conservation.

Integrating and Expanding Capacity and Capability: The SHC Framework challenges the Service to expand its capabilities for population/habitat modeling, landscape characterization and assessment, integrated monitoring, and biological information management at ecoregional scales. It challenges the Survey to in turn support the Service's efforts with its own growing capacity in these areas. In the realm of monitoring, SHC challenges the Service to link monitoring explicitly to decision-making. Within the realm of research, SHC challenges both agencies to modify existing processes for identifying research priorities to incorporate the documented assumptions and uncertainties that emanate from Biological Planning and Conservation Design.

Supporting Ecoregional Partnerships: The Service's emerging capabilities for SHC are typically occurring within the context of ecoregional-scale partnerships in which there is a strong focus on biological planning, conservation design, decision-based monitoring, and assumption-driven research. It is in the context of such partnerships that the Survey's growing capabilities in population/habitat modeling, landscape characterization and assessment, integrated monitoring, and bioinformatics can find their greatest relevance.

Creating Ecoregionally-based Conservation Science Teams: If SHC is to function as a framework that unifies the Service's conservation actions and the Survey's science support, it will require an operational construct. We envision that construct as being teams possibly organized as Conservation Science Offices, either real or virtual. A Conservation Science Office could be literal in the context of collocated employees or virtual in the sense of team members in separate stations. In each instance however, the team would consist of Service and Survey employees who cooperate to inform the efficient pursuit of Service goals and objectives for Federal trust resource conservation.

For those USGS employees that function as members of teams, the RGE processes should be modified to recognize the complexities of a science/management relationship that extends beyond the traditional research needs/response paradigm. Population/habitat models, landscape characterizations, biologically-driven decision support tools, statistically valid monitoring designs, etc. merit recognition as scholarly work essential to the Strategic Habitat Conservation Framework.

INTENT OF THE PARTIES

By entering into this MOU, the Regional Executive Leadership of both the Service and the Survey commit their respective regions to adopt procedures and protocols that support the functional elements of the SHC framework, and to develop (eco)regional Cooperative Agreements between FWS personnel responsible for ecoregional and landscape scale planning and assessment. and USGS personnel. These agreements should be developed and exercised in strategic locations and at strategic times in the future. Nothing in this MOU is intended to prohibit or discourage engaging other partners that may contribute to our collective capacity for SHC

One of the first steps in building a Service capacity for SHC is for Service Regions to explicitly define their goals for SHC and to develop strategies for attaining these goals. This will mean consulting with USGS to review existing assets in both bureaus, identifying priority areas for building SHC capacity, a draft timetable, and means of eventually juxtaposing existing or new staff with skills in Biological Planning, Conservation Design, Decision-based Monitoring and Assumption Driven Research (Attachment 1). Provisions for the development of (eco)regional Cooperative Agreements and the formation of conservation science teams should be prominent in Regional SHC strategies.

The Regional Executive Leadership are of one mind in stating that our intent extends beyond that of simply improving communication or coordination. Rather, it is one of creating new functional relationships between the Service and the Survey within each element of the SHC conservation framework. Our intent is that in the realm of federal trust resource conservation, both agencies move toward a collaborative Conservation Science Business Model.

PERIOD OF THE AGREEMENT: Progress in achieving the intent and purpose of the Agreement will be reviewed annually, and it will remain in effect until either party chooses to terminate its provisions or reassess its relevance.

SIGNATORS:

USFWS Regional Directors:

USGS Regional Directors:

ATTACHMENT 1
OVERVIEW OF FWS/USGS FUNCTIONAL ROLES AND RELATIONSHIPS
IN THE STRATEGIC HABITAT CONSERVATION FRAMEWORK

In the interest of fostering and furthering the Service-USGS relationship envisioned by the Strategic Habitat Conservation Framework and its associated Memorandum of Understanding, this Attachment provides guidance on the functional roles required of FWS and USGS. Science support requirements associated with each element are summarized, and the nature of the FWS/USGS relationship being sought is indicated. Service and USGS employees are also referred to the report "Strategic Habitat Conservation: A Report from the National Ecological Assessment Team" and the "Practitioner's Guide to Strategic Habitat Conservation" for additional details.

An array of functions is listed under each major SHC element (bold subheadings). Some of these roles are intrinsic to the Service. Others may logically be performed by USGS; however, as the agency mandated with Federal trust resource conservation, the Service is responsible for ensuring that each of these functions is accounted for in carrying out SHC.

Biological Planning: This Framework element encompasses the processes and procedures for deriving goals and objectives that reflect measurable biological outcomes linked across multiple spatial scales. It relies on transparent, replicable methods of population/habitat modeling and habitat characterization to assess the past, present, or forecasted ability of ecological systems and landscapes to support priority species at prescribed levels. Effective biological planning documents state testable hypotheses based on the assumptions upon which management operates and as such is critical to any adaptive conservation framework.

> Essential Functions:
> - Establish goals and objectives – this is an intrinsic Service role.
> - Document assumptions regarding limiting factors at site and landscape scales.
> - Developing models of measurable population-habitat relationships for priority Federal trust species.
> - Develop and refine earth resource (spatial) data sets essential to characterizing landscape attributes at ecoregional scales, e.g. wetlands (the NWI), land use/land cover, ecological systems, surficial geology, elevation, hydrography, hydrology, etc. .
> - Document the biological assumptions integral to models of population-habitat relationships.

Key Relationship Sought: USGS scientists experienced in population/habitat modeling and in the application of earth resource data sets to ecological assessment providing technical support to FWS conservation biologists and natural resource planners responsible for biological planning at landscape and ecoregional scales.

Conservation Design: This functional element of the SHC framework speaks to the myriad processes and tasks of establishing spatially explicit conservation priorities. Its aim is to define in a spatially explicit manner the landscape conditions presumed or predicted to sustain federal trust resources at prescribed levels. Key products are decision support models and maps of environmental sensitivity that support conservation delivery in achieving measurable biological outcomes.

Essential Functions:
- Engage private, state, federal conservation partners in defining spatially explicit conservation priorities – this is an intrinsic Service role.
- Document the biological assumptions integral to mapping environmental sensitivity and developing decision support tools.
- Provide information that supports the conservation community in targeting conservation programs in support of sustainable landscapes.
- Develop spatial application tools that support landscape characterization and accomplishment assessment by applying population/habitat models.
- Develop conservation decision support applications that allow partners to access and apply conservation strategies.
- Developing applications that allow the Service and its partners to track spatially the implementation of conservation practices and programs.

Key Relationship Sought: 1) USGS scientists experienced in population/habitat relationships providing technical support to FWS conservation biologists responsible for the development and application of decision support tools; and 2) USGS scientists experienced in IT applications providing technical support to FWS conservation biologists responsible for managing the conservation data integral to partner-driven, multi-scale conservation planning and assessment.

Decision-based Monitoring: This SHC functional element encompasses both the design and implementation of population and habitat monitoring programs tied to Service decision-making processes. Inventory and monitoring the Nation's biological resources is integral to the mission of both bureaus. Within this element of the SHC framework, the focus is on USGS providing technical assistance specific to Service responsibilities for monitoring and for integrating monitoring results into decision-making processes.

Essential Functions:
- Link any and all monitoring programs to specific decision-making processes.
- Ensure that monitoring activities at a project or landscape scale are contributing to ecoregional or national-scale monitoring programs wherever possible.
- Support establishment of the biological objectives of individual monitoring programs with respect to baseline inventorying, assessing trends, evaluating management prescriptions, or testing assumptions.
- Develop biologically sound monitoring protocols and statistically valid sampling frameworks.
- Develop protocols and procedures for data collection, storage, retrieval, and dissemination.
- Integrate FWS monitoring efforts with USGS national data bases and monitoring programs.

<u>Key Relationship Sought</u>: 1) USGS scientists experienced in population and habitat monitoring assisting FWS biologists whose duties include developing and implementing monitoring programs at both the project scale (individual Refuge) and at landscape/ecoregional scales in developing statistically valid sampling frameworks and monitoring protocols to 2) USGS scientists experienced in database development and management providing IT support to FWS conservation biologists and IT personnel responsible for managing the conservation data integral to partner-driven, multi-scale conservation planning and assessment.

Assumption-driven Research: This functional element acknowledges the need to progressively refine biological goals and objectives with research directed at testing the biological assumptions and uncertainties integral to science-based planning and assessment. Within the SHC Framework, biological planning and conservation design are Service responsibilities and each leads to explicitly stated assumptions regarding how site-scale actions are presumed or predicted to affect sustainability at higher spatial scales. Accordingly, the overarching responsibility for defining the otherwise implicit assumptions associated with its conservation actions rests with the Service.

<u>Essential Functions:</u>
- Define implicit assumptions associated with Service conservation actions.
- Identify and prioritize the key uncertainties associated with biological objectives, assessments of environmental sensitivity, or presumptions regarding biological response to conservation prescriptions or practices.
- Timely communication of results from research directed at the efficacy of assumptions.
- Refine population/habitat models and decision support tools based on knowledge gleaned from assumption-driven research.
- Translate basic assumptions into testable hypotheses.

<u>Key Relationship Sought</u>: FWS biologists responsible for biological planning and conservation design are assisted by USGS scientists in translating biological assumptions into testable hypotheses and prioritizing research based on the relative sensitivity of assumptions to FWS decision-making processes.

APPENDIX C

Technical Skills and Infrastructure Needs

In this appendix we recommend competencies and infrastructure to do the Biological Planning, Conservation Design, and Research and Monitoring elements of SHC.

Personnel

In building capacity for SHC, development of some form of "team" whereby coordination of scientific and GIS functions occurs is probably eventually essential. It may not be necessary for each program to contribute staff to these teams, but if true cross program coordination is the goal, it is necessary for every program to participate, if only by relaying information needs.

Obtaining the services of staff with right mix of skills, and ensuring that they function effectively as a team is essential. This capacity will generally be internal to the Service and USGS since SHC is on-going and not sporadic.

Staff are more likely to function effectively as a team if they (1) are co-located; (2) have a single team leader and/or the smallest possible number of direct supervisors; and (3) are made up of dedicated staff rather than staff participating as a collateral duty. Obviously it is not always possible to assemble a team of dedicated staff in one locations, under a single supervisor, but this is probably the optimal model.

Biological planning, conservation design, and research and monitoring are collectively an applied science endeavor; however, a mix of competencies is required for success (Table 1). These include:

1. Biological/ecological expertise
2. Knowledge of (specific) ecosystem characteristics
3. Spatial Analysis (GIS and image analysis)
4. Knowledge of habitat management practices
5. Statistical analysis
6. Research and monitoring design
7. Modeling techniques
8. Communication
9. Partnership building
10. Office Administration

It is less important how the services of staff with these competencies are obtained so long as they function effectively together.

Technical Infrastructure

Teams have relatively few specialized infrastructure needs. Computing needs including large amounts of hard disk space, RAM, and high processing speeds are available in most modern high end desktop computers. In most offices, computers, printers, networks, etc. can serve both as GIS platforms and for word processing and other routine office functions. More specialized hardware and software needs will generally include a:

1. large format plotter
2. high volume data backup system
3. GIS and statistical analysis software

Costs for spatial data and research and monitoring are situational but may be substantial; yet these are unavoidable costs of being a science-based agency. The important thing is to acquire quality data and to keep costs down by working cross-programmatically and with partners who will often have the same basic information needs. It is also important to remember that an agency like the Service does not develop a full-fledged capacity for SHC overnight. We will constantly strive to acquire better information and greater capacity; however, it is important to make the best use of existing information, capacity, and techniques at any given time.

Table 1. SHC technical functions and the competencies necessary to fulfill them.

Technical Functions	Competencies
Biological Planning	
Identify priority species	Knowledge of ecosystem characteristics
Assign species to guilds and select focal species	Biological/ecological expertise
Develop population objectives	Biological/ecological expertise and partnership skills
Identify limiting factors	Biological/ecological expertise
Compile empirical models	Biological/ecological expertise
	Knowledge of statistical analysis (modeling)
Compile conceptual models	Biological/ecological expertise
	Partnership or facilitation skills (modeling)
Assess current capacity of the ecoregion	Spatial analysis skills
Assess historic capacity of the ecoregion	Spatial analysis skills
Conservation Design	
Apply models to spatial data to develop Decision Support Tools	Spatial analysis skills
Identify program priority areas	Spatial analysis skills
	Knowledge of habitat management practices
Develop habitat objectives	Spatial analysis skills
	Knowledge of habitat management practices
Spatial data development	Spatial data development and management skills -

	possibly including satellite image analysis, photointerpretation
Support Conservation Delivery	
Work with managers in Service and	Knowledge of habitat management practices
partner agencies	Partnership building and management skills
Research and Monitoring	
Conduct targeted research	Research design, data analysis and communication skills
Monitor habitat response to management	Monitoring design and data analysis (monitoring) skills
	Knowledge of habitat management practices
Monitor population response to habitat	Monitoring design and data analysis (monitoring) skills
Assess progress toward population objectives	Monitoring design, model development, and spatial analysis skills
Evaluate program accomplishments	Monitoring design, model development, and spatial analysis skills
Logistics	
Office administration	Budget, personnel and property management
Partnership coordination	Communication and coordination skills, other partnership skills

Appendix D

Workforce Development in Biological Planning and Evaluation

Justification: Although the Service has a strong heritage as a science-based agency, we have established a goal of more systematically integrating science into our resource management programs through biological planning, conservation design and monitoring and research (hereafter, conservation assessment or CA). In this appendix, we propose one means of building CA capacity within the Service.

Narrative: Even working in close partnership with USGS, the Service will not build its needed capacity for CA overnight because program resources are limiting. Instead, conservation assessment teams will start out as small, nuclei of CA capacity. Over time, as CA becomes a standard element of our approach to conservation, as program resources allow, and as demand from managers for CA products increase, nuclear teams will expand and new teams will be established. In fact, as the NEAT acknowledged in this report, this growth in capacity is already occurring.

As demand for CA practitioners increases, teams will begin to compete with each other for the best and the brightest. Even now, migratory bird joint ventures eye each other warily over the prospect of loosing their most skilled CA practitioners to each other. One reason is that CA is among the most applied manifestations of science – biologists, spatial analysts, and statisticians must be able to work as a team and have an applied understanding of what others do. All must understand the needs and constraints of management, and must be able to think about management information needs at multiple, inter-related spatial scales. Thus, a planned approach to increasing workforce capacity for CA is necessary.

Proposal: One solution to this problem is a to develop a 1-2 year Internship Program wherein a Trainee is brought into an existing CA team and is "indoctrinated" into CA principles and processes and their technical skills are augmented as they experience enough of the "real world" of management that they will be able to perform independently, using proven processes, in another part of the country. Training objectives should be established for each Trainee based on their background as they work on a project that benefits the host team.

At the conclusion of a satisfactory internship, the Trainee would be eligible for non-competitive employment at another duty station (ideally in a new, forming CA team). Thus, in some respects, this proposal is similar to the SCEP, although the Trainee would not be a student and would work full time as a Service term employee.

Although the NEAT was not charged with resolving details associated with such a program, we suggest the following concerns and possible solutions.

Concern: Selection of the right Trainee will likely determine future success.

Solution: Trainee selection should be made by the host team – they have a proven track record for selecting individuals for this type of work and will be responsible for the trainee's performance.

Concern: Training would be a burden on host team staff and resources.
Solution: During the internship, the Trainee would conduct meaningful work that benefits the host team and incorporates the skills required to be successful at a future duty station. The program must be beneficial to the host team, Trainee, and the future duty station.

Concern: An effective internship will last too long and the future station will not want to wait.
Solution: The need must be identified early enough to accommodate a training period. A strategic plan for building SHC capacity is needed. Such a plan should incorporate increases in the size and number of teams and will be the foundation for implementing a CA Internship Program.

Concern: The Trainee may not be willing to move to a duty station.
Solution: Include the future duty station in the vacancy announcement, and make the Trainee aware of the conditions of participation, that is, a guarantee of permanent status only if they accept the position offered at the conclusion of the internship.

Geospatial Data and Technology Recommendations

There are significant opportunities to use the same or consistent geospatial data, GIS tools, and spatial analytical models in different applications and different locales that are each employing the basic conservation assessment methodologies described in this report. One key objective is to ensure that spatial data, tools, and models are: 1) developed according to consistent standards and practices, 2) well documented so that other practitioners may find and use them, and 3) made widely available through a web-accessible "library" or portal.

There are also potential efficiencies to be gained by providing joint (Service-wide) GIS technical training and technical support services that are geared to specific conservation assessment functions. Finally, there are some related geospatial data initiatives at the Department level which we believe can be leveraged to help support NEAT objectives. These include the DOI Enterprise Geographic Information Management (EGIM) activity, the development of a DOI-wide "Geospatial Modernization Blueprint" as a key part of the DOI Enterprise Information Architecture, and DOI leadership of the Geospatial One-Stop E-Government Initiative. FWS and USGS are playing lead roles in each of these multi-Bureau initiatives.

Implementation Recommendation 1: Establish national and ecoregional inter-bureau teams to identify and prioritize base data needs to facilitate Strategic Habitat Conservation (SHC) and support cost-effective, collaborative data acquisition efforts.

Implementing a capability for conservation assessment will require access to current geospatial data of appropriate scale and resolution. These data needs fall generally within two major categories: specified base data layers (e.g., elevation, hydrography, soils) which, in turn, provide a generic foundation or framework for focused thematic data layers (vegetation, species distribution, protected areas). A key immediate implementation recommendation therefore is to identify all the data needs in these two categories, specifying the preferred scales, resolutions, etc. for each key data set or layer. This set of consistently described data requirements can then be used to: 1) identify any *existing* data (from USGS and from other sources) that can be made available in a shared and consistent fashion to meet identified needs and 2) documenting the high priority *unmet* data needs so that these data needs can be shared with potential partners and collaborators in FWS, USGS, and in other agencies and organizations. This will encourage cost-sharing acquisition of data of mutual interest and leveraging of new data acquisition plans to meet conservation assessment needs.

USGS has lead responsibility for developing and maintaining current, high-resolution base geospatial data layers (including elevation, hydrography, and digital orthoimagery) for *The National Map*. This is primarily accomplished through partnerships and collaborations with Federal, State, and local government agencies. Another immediate implementation recommendation is to request that USGS, in developing its annual base geospatial data acquisition priorities, give full consideration, to the greatest extent possible, to addressing the base data needs and priorities of FWS, as associated with conservation assessment efforts.

Implementation Recommendation 2: Establish national and ecoregional inter-bureau teams to insure that data conform to required standards, are relevant to the region(s) that collect them, and facilitate cross-regional coordination on SHC.

Consistent data and replicable processes are important elements in science-based conservation activities. In order to have consistent data, data standards need to exist and be followed. FWS already has a data standards process for creating new standards or adopting existing standards used by groups such as the FGDC. Part of that process involves having a responsible data steward for each data standard, to shepherd the standard through the process and act as a subject matter expert.

Staff members at any centers applying science-based conservation are likely to be leaders in their subject areas and would make logical data stewards for new standards. They should also support the use of existing standards, such as the metadata standard.

Implementation Recommendation 3: Provide Mechanism for Developing, Documenting, and Sharing Common GIS Tools and Models Among Conservation Assessment Practitioners.

As GIS applications, tools, and geospatial models are developed, there should be a mechanism through which these tools, applications, and models can be readily shared with other conservation assessment practitioners so that they can be re-used and adapted as necessary. The objective is to avoid having individuals developing similar or redundant applications, when a usable tool already exists. This can be done by providing a web-based "library" of tools, applications, and models through which people can find and download those that meet their needs. Individual can also post new applications they have developed to the "library" to be shared with others. For this type of system to be effective, it will require the development of standardized metadata to describe or document each tool or model.

Implementation Recommendation 4: Identify hardware, bandwidth, and other technical infrastructure requirements at any physical team locations such as the Joint Venture offices.

The analysis and sharing of geospatial data requires larger hardware and wider bandwidth than computer applications such as e-mail or basic web connectivity. Interactive data sharing also has specific security requirements that are not normally present. The Service's IT infrastructure in general has been planned and sized to meet average requirements, not the outlying higher end requirements. When an office location is designated to do conservation assessment, technical infrastructure needs should be specified as soon as possible. There should never be the assumption that the Service's IT infrastructure can simply accommodate the increased needs for this type of work. Technical infrastructure requirements also include ensuring the necessary IT technical support (software and hardware installation, operation, and troubleshooting) is available to meet practitioner needs. Opportunities to build on and leverage the Service's existing Bureau-level IT technical support network to support these additional requirements should be explored, but it is likely that additional IT technical support resources will be needed, beyond current levels.

USGS may be able to supply information on the technical requirements for certain analysis or data sharing actions if their offices are already implementing those actions.

Implementation Recommendation 5: Identify topics for joint training opportunities, such as metadata, advanced GIS applications, and advanced software technical support.

Shared training is an area that can be implemented immediately. There are existing opportunities for metadata training that could easily be expanded to locations involved in SHC related data acquisition and creation. Documenting data and GIS tools and models that will be shared and reused by a number of staff is recognized as an important activity, but it is often pushed to the bottom of the priority list. Appropriate training can make it easier to create metadata and understand the importance of doing so.

There are other technical areas that seem to be excellent candidates for joint training. These might include specialized remote sensing applications for creation of land cover or vegetation data layers; field data collection methodology - with or without GPS units; or advanced GIS analysis and modeling techniques. In addition, there will be opportunities for joint training on advanced GIS software installation, maintenance, and use. The skills needed to create and maintain centers for data analysis and sharing go well beyond the usual GIS skills; effective coordination of training and on-going technical support for those skills would reduce costs and maximize the use of available staff resources.

Specific topics can be identified as the program develops, but the commitment to do joint training should be made at the start. The facilities at the National Conservation Training Center, the USGS Training Center in Denver, efforts of the DOI Enterprise Geographic Information Management (EGIM) team to coordinate DOI-wide training and the current USGS metadata training program should all be leveraged in this effort.

www.ingramcontent.com/pod-product-compliance
Lightning Source LLC
Chambersburg PA
CBHW081125280526
45787CB00007B/2982

* 9 781507 642481 *